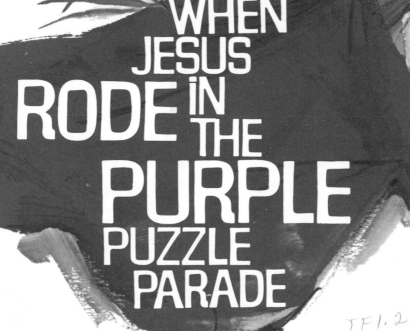

WHEN JESUS RODE IN THE PURPLE PUZZLE PARADE

Words by Norman C. Habel

Pictures by Jim Roberts

P A PURPLE PUZZLE TREE BOOK

COPYRIGHT © 1973 CONCORDIA PUBLISHING HOUSE, ST. LOUIS, MISSOURI
CONCORDIA PUBLISHING HOUSE LTD., LONDON, E. C. 1
MANUFACTURED IN THE UNITED STATES OF AMERICA
ALL RIGHTS RESERVED

ISBN 0-570-06546-1

Concordia Publishing House

Have you ever seen a wild parade
where trumpets, drums, and bugles play
to tell the whole, wide world
that on this day, this very day,
someone important is coming?

Have you seen bright banners fly
or jet planes write across the sky:
"A star is on his way?"
Then soon, soon, soon
with ticker tape and red balloons
he's really close to you.

Well, the purple puzzle parade
on the day that Jesus came to town
was nothing like that at all.
For Jesus didn't come to be a star,
a superduper movie star.
Far from it, my friend.

He was the purple puzzle King
who came to town to die;
to die alone
instead of ruling on a big red,
tall red, velvet cushion throne!

As the people marched along the road
that led to old Jerusalem,
they came to Jericho.

And there beside the road
a blind old beggar sat and cried,
"Son of David, have mercy on me!"

"What do you want from Me?" said Jesus.
"Do you want to join the big parade?"

"Master, I want to see," he said,
"I really want to see."
 Then Jesus said, "O.K.
 Because you trust in Me,
 open your eyes and go your way."

Well, the blind man's eyes were opened
and he led that big parade.
He danced along with lepers and fools,
with beggars and dogs,
and cripples that Jesus had healed
all along the road.

A little further down the road
Jesus gave a special order
to two of His disciples:
"Go to that village over there
and get Me a fresh, young donkey
that no one has ridden before."

When the dancing donkey arrived,
the beggars took their raggy robes
and threw them on his back
for Jesus to ride in style.
Others took their shaggy shirts
and waved them in the air like banners.
Some threw clothes across the road
to make a carpet full of colors
for the purple puzzle King
in that wild purple puzzle parade.

That purple puzzle donkey
flopped and danced along
with the beggars and their dogs.
And if you'd have been there with him
you might have heard his song:

Flop dingle, ding flopple,
dance dingaling!
Flop dingle, ding flopple,
dance dingaling!

Some people even ripped off branches,
long, sweeping, palm branches,
and swirled them through the air.
"Three cheers! Three cheers!" the people
cried.
"Hosanna to the Son of David.
Hosanna to our God on high."

Did Jesus look like a real king
with a royal robe and a crown?
Was He riding in a chariot
with a band of soldiers all His own?

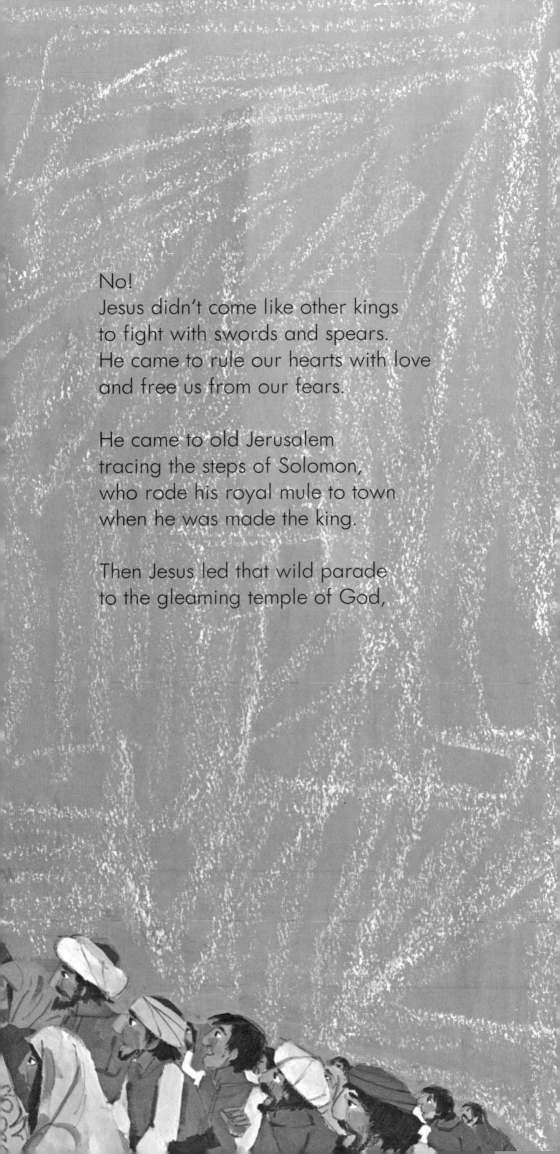

No!
Jesus didn't come like other kings
to fight with swords and spears.
He came to rule our hearts with love
and free us from our fears.

He came to old Jerusalem
tracing the steps of Solomon,
who rode his royal mule to town
when he was made the king.

Then Jesus led that wild parade
to the gleaming temple of God,

When Jesus went inside the temple
He didn't find the crowd
praising God for all His love.
Instead, He found them selling doves
that cried aloud for help.
"COOO COOO COOO," they cried,
"this place is worse than a zoo."

Then Jesus grabbed a heavy whip
with long, thin leather lashes
and swirled it round His head:
SSSSH SSSSH SSSSH
CRRRRRRRACK!

The greedy old salesmen
scrambled away in the corners,
and Jesus sent the tables flying
like papers in a storm.
Coins went spinning round their feet
and pigeons round their head.
"This is the house of God
and not a robber's cave," He said.
"You have turned a house of prayer
into a hole for filthy trade."

"You clumsy carpenter," the priests replied,
"why did You make this mess?
Give us a sign from God Himself
that You are right to do all this."

Jesus replied, "Just open your eyes!
The lame, the deaf, and the blind
have found new hope from Me.
And the children here in the temple
know I am the purple puzzle King
who came to set them free.
You try to keep them quiet.
I want to hear them sing."

And so the children sang that day
a song that sounds like this:

On Passover, if you were king,
would you let God's people swing?
Would you let them laugh and sing,
if you were king?

If you were king, do you believe
that you would have a New Year's Eve
with choc'late whistles up your sleeve,
if you were king?

And would you solve a mystery
like the purple puzzle tree,
and touch our hearts to set us free,
if you were king?

OTHER TITLES

SET I

WHEN GOD WAS ALL ALONE 56-1200
WHEN THE FIRST MAN CAME 56-1201
IN THE ENCHANTED GARDEN 56-1202
WHEN THE PURPLE WATERS CAME AGAIN 56-1203
IN THE LAND OF THE GREAT WHITE CASTLE 56-1204
WHEN LAUGHING BOY WAS BORN 56-1205
SET I LP RECORD 79-2200
SET I GIFT BOX (6 BOOKS, 1 RECORD) 56-1206

SET II

HOW TRICKY JACOB WAS TRICKED 56-1207
WHEN JACOB BURIED HIS TREASURE 56-1208
WHEN GOD TOLD US HIS NAME 56-1209
IS THAT GOD AT THE DOOR? 56-1210
IN THE MIDDLE OF A WILD CHASE 56-1211
THIS OLD MAN CALLED MOSES 56-1212
SET II LP RECORD 79-2201
SET II GIFT BOX (6 BOOKS, 1 RECORD) 56-1213

SET III

THE TROUBLE WITH TICKLE THE TIGER 56-1218
AT THE BATTLE OF JERICHO! HO! HO! 56-1219
GOD IS NOT A JACK-IN-A-BOX 56-1220
A LITTLE BOY WHO HAD A LITTLE FLING 56-1221
THE KING WHO WAS A CLOWN 56-1222
SING A SONG OF SOLOMON 56-1223
SET III LP RECORD 79-2202
SET III GIFT BOX (6 BOOKS, 1 RECORD) 56-1224

SET IV

ELIJAH AND THE BULL-GOD BAAL 56-1225
LONELY ELIJAH AND THE LITTLE PEOPLE 56-1226
WHEN ISAIAH SAW THE SIZZLING SERAPHIM 56-1227
A VOYAGE TO THE BOTTOM OF THE SEA 56-1228
WHEN JEREMIAH LEARNED A SECRET 56-1229
THE CLUMSY ANGEL AND THE NEW KING 56-1230
SET IV LP RECORD 79-2203
SET IV GIFT BOX (6 BOOKS, 1 RECORD) 56-1231

SET V

THE FIRST TRUE SUPER STAR 56-1242
A WILD YOUNG MAN CALLED JOHN 56-1243
THE DIRTY DEVIL AND THE CARPENTERS BOY 56-1244
WHEN JESUS DID HIS MIRACLES OF LOVE 56-1245
WHEN JESUS TOLD HIS PARABLES 56-1246
OLD ROCK THE FISHERMAN 56-1247
SET V LP RECORD 79-2204
SET V GIFT BOX 56-1248

SET VI

WONDER BREAD FROM A BOY'S LUNCH 56-1249
WHEN JESUS RODE IN THE PURPLE PUZZLE
PARADE 56-1250
WHEN JESUS' FRIENDS BETRAYED HIM 56-1251
THE DEEP DARK DAY WHEN JESUS DIED 56-1252
DANCE, LITTLE ALLELU, WITH ME 56-1253
THE KEY TO THE PURPLE PUZZLE TREE 56-1254
SET VI LP RECORD 79-2205
SET VI GIFT BOX 56-1255

the PURPLE PUZZLE TREE